I Love
Crocodiles

By Steve Parker
Illustrated by Steve Roberts

Miles
KeLLY

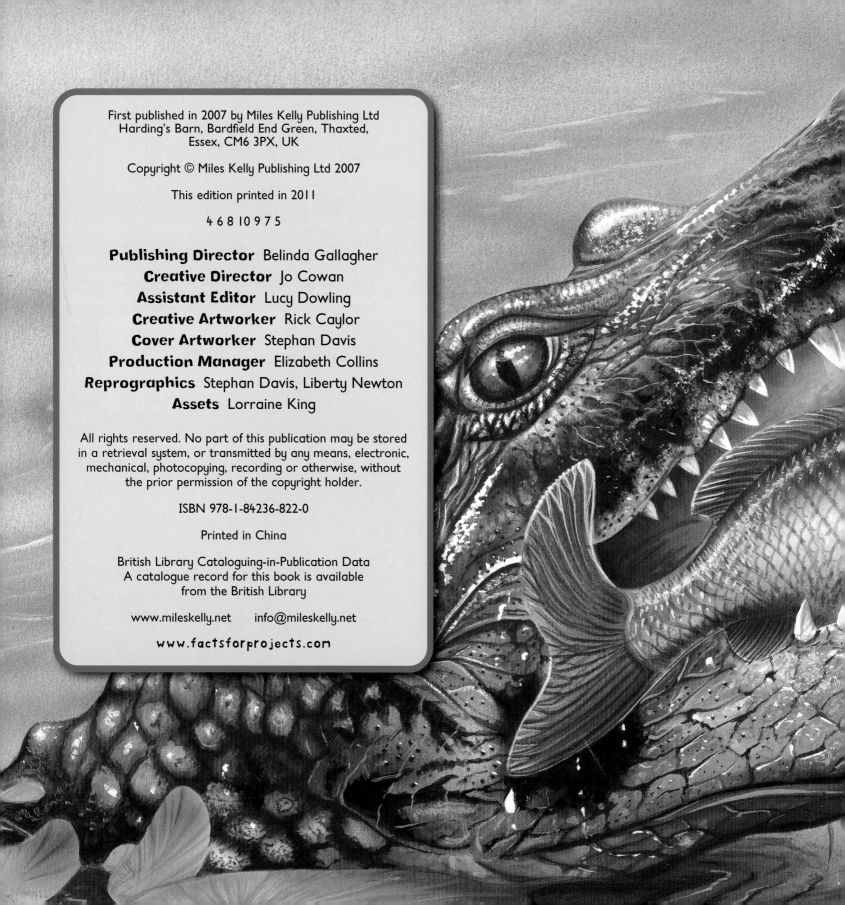

First published in 2007 by Miles Kelly Publishing Ltd
Harding's Barn, Bardfield End Green, Thaxted,
Essex, CM6 3PX, UK

Copyright © Miles Kelly Publishing Ltd 2007

This edition printed in 2011

4 6 8 10 9 7 5

Publishing Director Belinda Gallagher
Creative Director Jo Cowan
Assistant Editor Lucy Dowling
Creative Artworker Rick Caylor
Cover Artworker Stephan Davis
Production Manager Elizabeth Collins
Reprographics Stephan Davis, Liberty Newton
Assets Lorraine King

ISBN 978-1-84236-822-0

Printed in China

British Library Cataloguing-in-Publication Data
A catalogue record for this book is available
from the British Library

www.mileskelly.net   info@mileskelly.net

www.factsforprojects.com

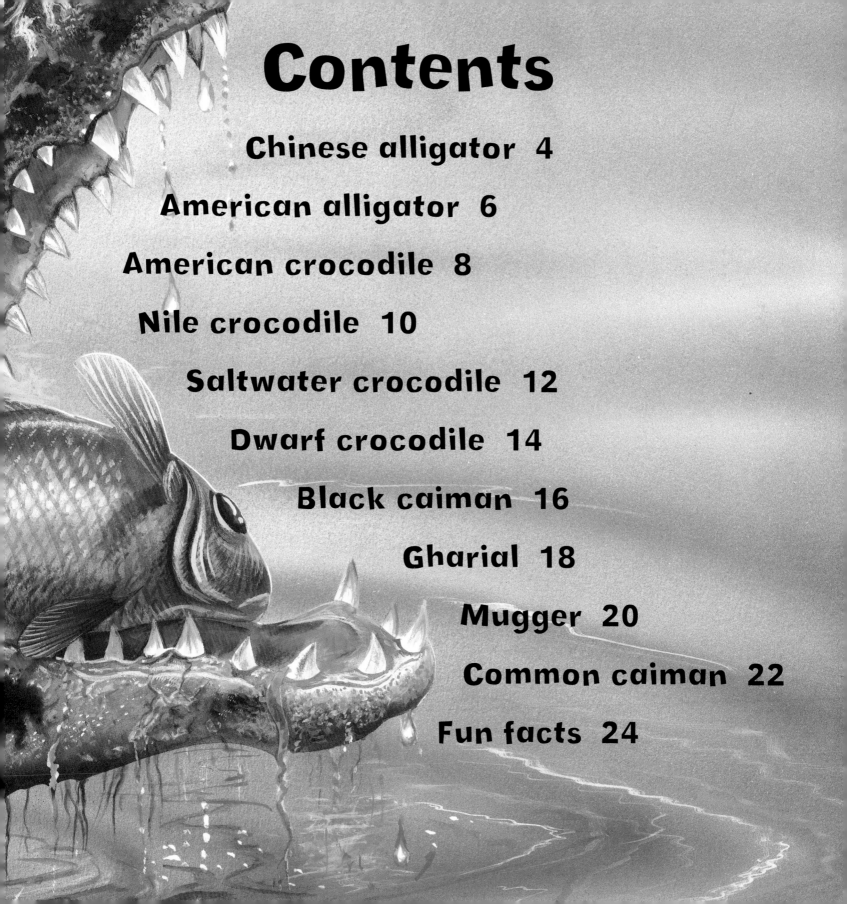

Contents

Chinese alligator

Crocodiles and alligators do not move about quickly. They are still for much of the time, as they soak up the sun and watch for food. If the weather is cold, crocodiles lie still because they are too cool to move. The Chinese alligator is still all winter. It sleeps in a cave or burrow and wakes up in spring.

Rarest of all

There are not many Chinese alligators left in the world. There may be as few as 150 living in the wild.

From October to March, the Chinese alligator sleeps to avoid the cold weather. When it wakes up, it is very hungry!

The Chinese alligator is one of the smallest members of the crocodile family. It is less than 2 metres in length.

This alligator uses its teeth to crush tough food. It eats snails, clams, crabs and other shelled creatures.

American alligator

The female American alligator is a caring mother. She makes a huge pile of mud and plants, lays her 40 to 50 eggs inside, and guards them well. When the babies are ready to hatch, they squeak inside their egg shells. Their mother carefully digs them out.

When the baby alligator hatches, its first meal will probably be a water insect or baby fish.

The alligator's nest is made from rotting plants. As they rot, the plants make heat that keeps the eggs warm.

The female alligator carefully pulls each egg from the nest so that the baby can break out of its egg shell.

Caring mums!
Like most crocodile and alligator mothers, the American alligator guards her eggs and babies fiercely.

American crocodile

The American crocodile spends most of its time doing nothing. It lies on the riverbank or floats in the water. This is part of its hunting method. Animals wander past, stop to drink, and SNAP! They get dragged into the water and eaten!

American crocodiles gather in groups when there is lots of food to eat.

As a crocodile floats in water, its eyes, ears and nose are above the surface. It then lies and waits for its next meal.

Old Croc!

Crocodiles live to a great age – if they stay out of trouble. The older they are, the longer they grow. Some are over 100 years old!

If the weather is cool, crocodiles can only move slowly. After they warm up by lying in the sun, they can run as fast as you can!

Nile crocodile

One of the most dangerous crocodiles is the Nile crocodile. Each year it kills more people in Africa than lions do! Luckily, after a big meal, a crocodile can last for a month or two before it's hungry again.

The Nile crocodile waits in the muddy water for a thirsty animal to come and drink.

Croc farms
Well-fed crocodiles living on farms grow almost twice as fast as those in the wild.

Many crocodiles swallow stones to make themselves heavier. Then they can float unseen, just below the water's surface.

When a crocodile relaxes with its mouth wide open, small birds pick its teeth clean – and get a meal of their own.

Saltwater crocodile

The saltwater crocodile is the biggest reptile in the world. It is far larger than any snake, lizard, turtle or tortoise. In fact, it is powerful enough to catch all kinds of animals, from small fish to large deer – even animals as big as you!

The saltwater crocodile has two rows of tall scales along its back.

Saltwater crocodiles live in swamps, rivers and lakes. They are fierce and dangerous, especially if surprised or cornered.

All crocodiles and alligators have five toes on each front foot, and four toes on each back foot.

Seaside croc!
The saltwater crocodile gets its name because it lives in rivers and lakes, but it can also swim out to sea.

Dwarf crocodile

One of the smallest crocodiles is the dwarf crocodile. It is just 1.5 metres long. In fact, it is so small that one frog is a big feast! This crocodile does not like to sit in the sunshine. Instead, it hides among plants by day and comes out to hunt at night.

There are two kinds of dwarf crocodile and both live in Africa. These crocodiles can live for 50 to 100 years.

Swish that tail
Hold your hand on its edge in water, and swish it to and fro. This is how a crocodile uses its tail to swim. A flat hand has less power.

Although it is small, the dwarf crocodile is very well protected. It has lots of thick scales all over its body – even on its eyelids.

The dwarf crocodile is also called the short-snouted crocodile, because its nose and jaws are not very long.

15

Black caiman

Like other crocodiles and alligators, the black caiman grows a new tooth almost every week. The old teeth get worn, chipped and broken, and fall out one by one. Each time, a new tooth grows from inside the jaw to replace the lost one. A crocodile is never toothless!

Caimans are a type of alligator. There are five different kinds of caiman and they all live in Central and South America.

Dino-crocs

Crocodiles were around before the dinosaurs, over 200 million years ago. Some were as long as three cars.

Black caimans are not all black. They have patterns of white spots, and grey and yellow patches, on a brown or black background.

The black caiman eats lots of different animals, including large fish, turtles and water snakes.

Gharial

The gharial breathes air into its lungs, like other crocodiles. It can hold its breath and stay underwater for a long time – more than half an hour. Gharials can also hunt underwater, and even eat their food there.

Gharials spend a lot of time in the water chasing fish. They do not move about on land as much as other crocodiles.

The gharial's long snout is very thin. It has lots of small, pointed teeth – perfect for catching slippery fish.

Bumpy nose!
The male gharial has a lump on the front of its nose, at the tip. The female gharial does not.

To swim fast, crocodiles move their tails from side to side and steer with their feet.

Like all crocodiles, the gharial has flaps of skin called webs, between its toes.

19

Mugger

The mugger is a powerful crocodile that likes any kind of fresh water. It even hides in ditches and canals. In big lakes, it follows fishing boats and steals the fish from the nets! The mugger's jaws and teeth are strong enough to crush a turtle's shell, or drag a buffalo under the surface so that it drowns.

Like all crocodiles and alligators, the mugger has tough thick scales covering its body.

A young mugger has
dark stripes across
its body and tail.
These fade as it
gets older.

Walk like a croc

Try walking like a crocodile,
with your arms and legs on
the floor beneath your body.

Common caiman

The common caiman likes any fresh water, from lakes and rivers, to canals and ditches. It even lies in the water troughs that people put out for farm animals. When they come for a drink – SNAP!

The common caiman has a bony ridge in front of each eye. It looks as if it is wearing glasses.

Caimans catch fish, water birds and river snails. They even eat piranhas – fierce fish with sharp teeth.

These caimans have the toughest body scales of almost any crocodile. Each scale is as thick and tough as the heel of a boot.

On the move
Common caimans prefer swampy areas, but will move around to live almost anywhere.

Fun facts

Chinese alligator This alligator is also known as the muddy dragon.

American alligator When it feels threatened, the American alligator uses its large tail as a weapon.

American crocodile Adult American crocodiles can stay underwater for 30 minutes.

Nile crocodile Female Nile crocodiles push each other out of the way in order to get the best nesting place.

Saltwater crocodile These crocodiles are able to swim great distances out to sea.

Dwarf crocodile The dwarf crocodile is becoming endangered as it is hunted for its skin.

Black caiman The female black caiman can lay between 50 and 60 eggs.

Gharial Although they are good swimmers, the gharial cannot walk very well on land.

Mugger Birds, monkeys, deer and even buffaloes are all tasty meals for muggers.

Common caiman The common caiman can be found living on tropical islands in the Caribbean.